School

Book Report

Journal

(for Fiction)

Name _____

Grade _____ Year _____

Teacher _____

Class _____

School _____

D1378923

School Book Report Journal (for Fiction)

Copyright © 2016 Zishka Journals

All rights reserved.

Zishka Publishing

www.zishkapublishing.com

Education. Language workbooks. Book reports.

ISBN-13: 978-1-941691-06-9

ISBN-10: 1-941691-06-4

Using This Journal

This journal is designed for writing book reports for stories for which the following fields apply:

Title: Enter the title of the book.

Author(s): List the authors of the book.

Publisher: Enter the name of the publishing company.

Publication Date: Enter the most recent publication date listed on the copyright page.

Genre(s)/Subject(s): What type of book is it? Examples include romance, mystery, science fiction, fantasy, horror, and historical.

Illustration: Draw a picture relating to the story. (For fantasy, it may be handy to draw a map.)

Primary Setting(s): Where does the story take place?

Time Period(s): When does the story take place?

Main Characters: List and describe the main characters. Identify the protagonist and antagonist.

Main Idea: Summarize the main idea of the story in one sentence.

Main Events: Briefly summarize the main events of the story.

Climax: Briefly describe the climax of the story. It's the turning point and decisive moment, usually occurring toward the end of the story.

Conflict & Resolution: Briefly describe the conflict in the story and how it was resolved.

Synopsis: Briefly summarize the plot.

Interpretation: Interpret a non-obvious element of the story, such as any symbolism used.

Quotes: Record your favorite lines from the story.

Vocabulary Words: List and define words from the story that you found challenging.

Notes: Use this space to record additional notes, or to continue previous sections.

Notes

You can adapt this book report journal to your specific needs:

- You don't need to complete every section (unless you're doing this for a class and that's what your teacher expects).
- You can cross out a section and replace it with another (with the same exception as previously noted).
- The Notes section can be used to continue a section if additional space is needed. Those who wish to write much more can attach extra sheets to a report.
- Teachers can assign specific sections, provide specific vocabulary words, replace some sections with others, or require additional writing in the Notes section or via attached sheets, for example.

BOOK REPORT #1

Title _____

Author(s) _____

Publisher _____ Publication Date _____

Genre(s)/Subject(s) _____

Illustration

Primary Setting(s) _____

Time Period(s) _____

Main Characters _____

_____

_____

_____

_____

Main Idea _____

_____

Main Events _____

_____

_____

Climax _____

_____

Conflict & Resolution _____

_____

_____

Synopsis _____

_____

_____

_____

_____

Interpretation _____

_____

_____

_____

What did you enjoy most about the story? _____

_____

What would you change about the story? _____

_____

Quotes

_____

_____

_____

_____

_____

_____

_____

_____

Vocabulary Words

_____

_____

_____

_____

Notes

_____

_____

_____

_____

_____

_____

_____

_____

_____

BOOK REPORT #2

Title _____

Author(s) _____

Publisher _____ Publication Date _____

Genre(s)/Subject(s) _____

Illustration

Primary Setting(s) _____

Time Period(s) _____

Main Characters _____

_____

_____

_____

_____

Main Idea _____

_____

Main Events _____

_____

_____

Climax _____

_____

Conflict & Resolution _____

_____

_____

Synopsis _____

_____

_____

_____

_____

Interpretation _____

_____

_____

_____

What did you enjoy most about the story? _____

_____

What would you change about the story? _____

_____

Quotes

_____

_____

_____

_____

_____

_____

_____

_____

_____

Vocabulary Words

_____

_____

_____

_____

Notes

_____

_____

_____

_____

_____

_____

_____

_____

_____

_____

BOOK REPORT #3

Title _____

Author(s) _____

Publisher _____ Publication Date _____

Genre(s)/Subject(s) _____

Illustration

Primary Setting(s) _____

Time Period(s) _____

Main Characters _____

_____

_____

_____

_____

Main Idea _____

_____

Main Events _____

_____

_____

Climax _____

_____

Conflict & Resolution _____

_____

_____

Synopsis _____

_____

_____

_____

_____

Interpretation _____

_____

_____

_____

What did you enjoy most about the story? _____

_____

What would you change about the story? _____

_____

Quotes

_____

_____

_____

_____

_____

_____

_____

_____

Vocabulary Words

_____

_____

_____

_____

_____

Notes

_____

_____

_____

_____

_____

_____

_____

_____

_____

_____

BOOK REPORT #4

Title _____

Author(s) _____

Publisher _____ Publication Date _____

Genre(s)/Subject(s) _____

Illustration

Primary Setting(s) _____

Time Period(s) _____

Main Characters _____

_____

_____

_____

_____

Main Idea _____

_____

Main Events _____

_____

_____

Climax _____

_____

Conflict & Resolution _____

_____

_____

Synopsis _____

_____

_____

_____

Interpretation _____

_____

_____

_____

What did you enjoy most about the story? _____

_____

What would you change about the story? _____

_____

Quotes

_____

_____

_____

_____

_____

_____

_____

_____

_____

Vocabulary Words

_____

_____

_____

_____

Notes

_____

_____

_____

_____

_____

_____

_____

_____

BOOK REPORT #5

Title _____

Author(s) _____

Publisher _____ Publication Date _____

Genre(s)/Subject(s) _____

Illustration

Primary Setting(s) _____

Time Period(s) _____

Main Characters _____

_____

_____

_____

Main Idea _____

_____

Main Events _____

_____

_____

Climax _____

_____

Conflict & Resolution _____

_____

_____

Synopsis _____

_____

_____

_____

_____

Interpretation _____

_____

_____

_____

What did you enjoy most about the story? _____

_____

What would you change about the story? _____

_____

Quotes

_____

_____

_____

_____

_____

_____

_____

_____

_____

Vocabulary Words

Notes

BOOK REPORT #6

Title _____

Author(s) _____

Publisher _____ Publication Date _____

Genre(s)/Subject(s) _____

Illustration

Primary Setting(s) _____

Time Period(s) _____

Main Characters _____

_____

_____

_____

Main Idea _____

_____

Main Events _____

_____

_____

Climax _____

_____

Conflict & Resolution _____

_____

_____

Synopsis _____

_____

_____

_____

_____

Interpretation _____

_____

_____

_____

What did you enjoy most about the story? _____

_____

What would you change about the story? _____

_____

Quotes

_____

_____

_____

_____

_____

_____

_____

_____

_____

Vocabulary Words

_____

_____

_____

_____

_____

Notes

_____

_____

_____

_____

_____

_____

_____

_____

_____

_____

BOOK REPORT #7

Title _____

Author(s) _____

Publisher _____ Publication Date _____

Genre(s)/Subject(s) _____

Illustration

Primary Setting(s) _____

Time Period(s) _____

Main Characters _____

_____

_____

_____

_____

Main Idea _____

_____

Main Events _____

_____

_____

Climax _____

_____

Conflict & Resolution _____

_____

_____

Synopsis _____

_____

_____

_____

_____

Interpretation _____

_____

_____

_____

What did you enjoy most about the story? _____

_____

What would you change about the story? _____

_____

Quotes

_____

_____

_____

_____

_____

_____

_____

_____

_____

Vocabulary Words

_____

_____

_____

_____

_____

Notes

_____

_____

_____

_____

_____

_____

_____

_____

_____

_____

BOOK REPORT #8

Title _____

Author(s) _____

Publisher _____ Publication Date _____

Genre(s)/Subject(s) _____

Illustration

Primary Setting(s) _____

Time Period(s) _____

Main Characters _____

_____

_____

_____

_____

Main Idea _____

_____

Main Events _____

_____

_____

Climax _____

_____

Conflict & Resolution _____

_____

_____

Synopsis _____

_____

_____

_____

_____

Interpretation _____

_____

_____

_____

What did you enjoy most about the story? _____

_____

What would you change about the story? _____

_____

Quotes

_____

_____

_____

_____

_____

_____

_____

_____

Vocabulary Words

_____

_____

_____

_____

Notes

_____

_____

_____

_____

_____

_____

_____

_____

_____

BOOK REPORT #9

Title _____

Author(s) _____

Publisher _____ Publication Date _____

Genre(s)/Subject(s) _____

Illustration

Primary Setting(s) _____

Time Period(s) _____

Main Characters _____

_____

_____

_____

_____

Main Idea _____

_____

Main Events _____

_____

_____

Climax _____

_____

Conflict & Resolution _____

_____

_____

Synopsis _____

_____

_____

_____

_____

Interpretation _____

_____

_____

_____

What did you enjoy most about the story? _____

_____

What would you change about the story? _____

_____

Quotes

_____

_____

_____

_____

_____

_____

_____

_____

_____

_____

Vocabulary Words

Notes

BOOK REPORT #10

Title _____

Author(s) _____

Publisher _____ Publication Date _____

Genre(s)/Subject(s) _____

Illustration

Primary Setting(s) _____

Time Period(s) _____

Main Characters _____

_____

_____

_____

_____

Main Idea _____

_____

Main Events _____

_____

_____

Climax _____

_____

Conflict & Resolution _____

_____

_____

Synopsis _____

_____

_____

_____

Interpretation _____

_____

_____

_____

What did you enjoy most about the story? _____

_____

What would you change about the story? _____

_____

Quotes

_____

_____

_____

_____

_____

_____

_____

_____

_____

_____

Vocabulary Words

_____

_____

_____

_____

_____

Notes

_____

_____

_____

_____

_____

_____

_____

_____

_____

_____

BOOK REPORT #11

Title _____

Author(s) _____

Publisher _____ Publication Date _____

Genre(s)/Subject(s) _____

Illustration

Primary Setting(s) _____

Time Period(s) _____

Main Characters _____

_____

_____

_____

_____

Main Idea _____

_____

Main Events _____

_____

_____

Climax _____

_____

Conflict & Resolution _____

_____

_____

Synopsis _____

_____

_____

_____

_____

Interpretation _____

_____

_____

_____

What did you enjoy most about the story? _____

_____

What would you change about the story? _____

_____

Quotes

_____

_____

_____

_____

_____

_____

_____

_____

_____

Vocabulary Words

_____

_____

_____

_____

_____

Notes

_____

_____

_____

_____

_____

_____

_____

_____

_____

_____

_____

BOOK REPORT #12

Title _____

Author(s) _____

Publisher _____ Publication Date _____

Genre(s)/Subject(s) _____

Illustration

Primary Setting(s) _____

Time Period(s) _____

Main Characters _____

_____

_____

_____

_____

Main Idea _____

_____

Main Events _____

_____

_____

Climax _____

_____

Conflict & Resolution _____

_____

_____

Synopsis _____

_____

_____

_____

_____

Interpretation _____

_____

_____

_____

What did you enjoy most about the story? _____

_____

What would you change about the story? _____

_____

Quotes

_____

_____

_____

_____

_____

_____

_____

_____

_____

Vocabulary Words

_____

_____

_____

_____

Notes

_____

_____

_____

_____

_____

_____

_____

BOOK REPORT #13

Title _____

Author(s) _____

Publisher _____ Publication Date _____

Genre(s)/Subject(s) _____

Illustration

Primary Setting(s) _____

Time Period(s) _____

Main Characters _____

_____

_____

_____

Main Idea _____

_____

Main Events _____

_____

_____

Climax _____

_____

Conflict & Resolution _____

_____

_____

Synopsis _____

_____

_____

_____

_____

Interpretation _____

_____

_____

_____

What did you enjoy most about the story? _____

_____

What would you change about the story? _____

_____

Quotes

_____

_____

_____

_____

_____

_____

_____

_____

_____

Vocabulary Words

_____

_____

_____

_____

_____

Notes

_____

_____

_____

_____

_____

_____

_____

_____

_____

_____

_____

BOOK REPORT #14

Title _____

Author(s) _____

Publisher _____ Publication Date _____

Genre(s)/Subject(s) _____

Illustration

Primary Setting(s) _____

Time Period(s) _____

Main Characters _____

_____

_____

_____

_____

Main Idea _____

_____

Main Events _____

_____

_____

Climax _____

_____

Conflict & Resolution _____

_____

_____

Synopsis _____

_____

_____

_____

Interpretation _____

_____

_____

_____

What did you enjoy most about the story? _____

_____

What would you change about the story? _____

_____

Quotes

_____

_____

_____

_____

_____

_____

_____

_____

_____

Vocabulary Words

_____

_____

_____

_____

_____

Notes

_____

_____

_____

_____

_____

_____

_____

_____

_____

_____

BOOK REPORT #15

Title _____

Author(s) _____

Publisher _____ Publication Date _____

Genre(s)/Subject(s) _____

Illustration

Primary Setting(s) _____

Time Period(s) _____

Main Characters _____

_____

_____

_____

_____

Main Idea _____

_____

Main Events _____

_____

_____

Climax _____

_____

Conflict & Resolution _____

_____

_____

Synopsis _____

_____

_____

_____

Interpretation _____

_____

_____

_____

What did you enjoy most about the story? _____

_____

What would you change about the story? _____

_____

Quotes

_____

_____

_____

_____

_____

_____

_____

_____

_____

Vocabulary Words

_____

_____

_____

_____

_____

Notes

_____

_____

_____

_____

_____

_____

_____

_____

_____

_____

BOOK REPORT #16

Title _____

Author(s) _____

Publisher _____ Publication Date _____

Genre(s)/Subject(s) _____

Illustration

Primary Setting(s) _____

Time Period(s) _____

Main Characters _____

_____

_____

_____

Main Idea _____

_____

Main Events _____

_____

_____

Climax _____

_____

Conflict & Resolution _____

_____

_____

Synopsis _____

_____

_____

_____

_____

Interpretation _____

_____

_____

_____

What did you enjoy most about the story? _____

_____

What would you change about the story? _____

_____

Quotes

_____

_____

_____

_____

_____

_____

_____

_____

_____

_____

Vocabulary Words

_____

_____

_____

_____

Notes

_____

_____

_____

_____

_____

_____

_____

_____

_____

_____

BOOK REPORT #17

Title _____

Author(s) _____

Publisher _____ Publication Date _____

Genre(s)/Subject(s) _____

Illustration

Primary Setting(s) _____

Time Period(s) _____

Main Characters _____

_____

_____

_____

_____

Main Idea _____

_____

Main Events _____

_____

_____

Climax _____

_____

Conflict & Resolution _____

_____

_____

Synopsis _____

_____

_____

_____

_____

Interpretation _____

_____

_____

_____

What did you enjoy most about the story? _____

_____

What would you change about the story? _____

_____

Quotes

_____

_____

_____

_____

_____

_____

_____

_____

Vocabulary Words

_____

_____

_____

_____

_____

Notes

_____

_____

_____

_____

_____

_____

_____

_____

_____

BOOK REPORT #18

Title _____

Author(s) _____

Publisher _____ Publication Date _____

Genre(s)/Subject(s) _____

Illustration

Primary Setting(s) _____

Time Period(s) _____

Main Characters _____

_____

_____

_____

Main Idea _____

_____

Main Events _____

_____

_____

Climax _____

_____

Conflict & Resolution _____

_____

_____

Synopsis _____

_____

_____

_____

Interpretation _____

_____

_____

_____

What did you enjoy most about the story? _____

_____

What would you change about the story? _____

_____

Quotes

_____

_____

_____

_____

_____

_____

_____

_____

_____

_____

Vocabulary Words

_____

_____

_____

_____

Notes

_____

_____

_____

_____

_____

_____

_____

_____

BOOK REPORT #19

Title _____

Author(s) _____

Publisher _____ Publication Date _____

Genre(s)/Subject(s) _____

Illustration

Primary Setting(s) _____

Time Period(s) _____

Main Characters _____

_____

_____

_____

_____

Main Idea _____

_____

Main Events _____

_____

_____

Climax _____

_____

Conflict & Resolution _____

_____

_____

Synopsis _____

_____

_____

_____

_____

Interpretation _____

_____

_____

_____

What did you enjoy most about the story? _____

_____

What would you change about the story? _____

_____

Quotes

_____

_____

_____

_____

_____

_____

_____

_____

_____

_____

Vocabulary Words

_____

_____

_____

_____

Notes

_____

_____

_____

_____

_____

_____

_____

_____

_____

_____

BOOK REPORT #20

Title _____

Author(s) _____

Publisher _____ Publication Date _____

Genre(s)/Subject(s) _____

Illustration

Primary Setting(s) _____

Time Period(s) _____

Main Characters _____

_____

_____

_____

_____

Main Idea _____

_____

Main Events _____

_____

_____

Climax _____

_____

Conflict & Resolution _____

_____

_____

Synopsis _____

_____

_____

_____

_____

Interpretation _____

_____

_____

_____

What did you enjoy most about the story? _____

_____

What would you change about the story? _____

_____

Quotes

_____

_____

_____

_____

_____

_____

_____

_____

_____

Vocabulary Words

Notes

BOOK REPORT #21

Title _____

Author(s) _____

Publisher _____ Publication Date _____

Genre(s)/Subject(s) _____

Illustration

Primary Setting(s) _____

Time Period(s) _____

Main Characters _____

_____

_____

_____

_____

Main Idea _____

_____

Main Events _____

_____

_____

Climax _____

_____

Conflict & Resolution _____

_____

_____

Synopsis _____

_____

_____

_____

_____

Interpretation _____

_____

_____

_____

What did you enjoy most about the story? _____

_____

What would you change about the story? _____

_____

Quotes

_____

_____

_____

_____

_____

_____

_____

_____

Vocabulary Words

_____

_____

_____

_____

_____

Notes

_____

_____

_____

_____

_____

_____

_____

_____

_____

_____

BOOK REPORT #22

Title _____

Author(s) _____

Publisher _____ Publication Date _____

Genre(s)/Subject(s) _____

Illustration

Primary Setting(s) _____

Time Period(s) _____

Main Characters _____

_____

_____

_____

_____

Main Idea _____

_____

Main Events _____

_____

_____

Climax _____

_____

Conflict & Resolution _____

_____

_____

Synopsis _____

_____

_____

_____

Interpretation _____

_____

_____

_____

What did you enjoy most about the story? _____

_____

What would you change about the story? _____

_____

Quotes

_____

_____

_____

_____

_____

_____

_____

_____

_____

Vocabulary Words

_____

_____

_____

_____

Notes

_____

_____

_____

_____

_____

_____

_____

_____

_____

_____

BOOK REPORT #23

Title _____

Author(s) _____

Publisher _____ Publication Date _____

Genre(s)/Subject(s) _____

Illustration

Primary Setting(s) _____

Time Period(s) _____

Main Characters _____

_____

_____

_____

Main Idea _____

_____

Main Events _____

_____

_____

Climax _____

_____

Conflict & Resolution _____

_____

_____

Synopsis _____

_____

_____

_____

Interpretation _____

_____

_____

_____

What did you enjoy most about the story? _____

_____

What would you change about the story? _____

_____

Quotes

_____

_____

_____

_____

_____

_____

_____

_____

_____

Vocabulary Words

_____

_____

_____

_____

Notes

_____

_____

_____

_____

_____

_____

_____

_____

_____

BOOK REPORT #24

Title _____

Author(s) _____

Publisher _____ Publication Date _____

Genre(s)/Subject(s) _____

Illustration

Primary Setting(s) _____

Time Period(s) _____

Main Characters _____

_____

_____

_____

Main Idea _____

_____

Main Events _____

_____

_____

Climax _____

_____

Conflict & Resolution _____

_____

_____

Synopsis _____

_____

_____

_____

Interpretation _____

_____

_____

_____

What did you enjoy most about the story? _____

_____

What would you change about the story? _____

_____

Quotes

_____

_____

_____

_____

_____

_____

_____

_____

_____

Vocabulary Words

_____

_____

_____

_____

Notes

_____

_____

_____

_____

_____

_____

_____

_____

_____

BOOK REPORT #25

Title _____

Author(s) _____

Publisher _____ Publication Date _____

Genre(s)/Subject(s) _____

Illustration

Primary Setting(s) _____

Time Period(s) _____

Main Characters _____

_____

_____

_____

Main Idea _____

_____

Main Events _____

_____

_____

Climax _____

_____

Conflict & Resolution _____

_____

_____

Synopsis _____

_____

_____

_____

_____

Interpretation _____

_____

_____

_____

What did you enjoy most about the story? _____

_____

What would you change about the story? _____

_____

Quotes

_____

_____

_____

_____

_____

_____

_____

_____

Vocabulary Words

_____

_____

_____

_____

Notes

_____

_____

_____

_____

_____

_____

_____

_____

_____